ATTACK OF THE KILLER BEES

BY EMILY MAHONEY

Gareth Stevens
PUBLISHING

e visit our website, www.garethstevens.com. For a free color catalog of all our high-quality books, call toll free 1-800-542-2595 or fax 1-877-542-2596.

Library of Congress Cataloging-in-Publication Data

Names: Mahoney, Emily Jankowski.
Title: Attack of the killer bees / Emily Mahoney.
Description: New York : Gareth Stevens Publishing, [2017] | Series: Animal invaders. Destroying native habitats | Includes index.
Identifiers: LCCN 2016037124| ISBN 9781482456608 (pbk. book) | ISBN 9781482456714 (6 pack) | ISBN 9781482456721 (library bound book)
Subjects: LCSH: Africanized honeybee–Juvenile literature. | Bees–Juvenile literature.
Classification: LCC QL568.A6 M5115 2017 | DDC 595.79/9–dc23
LC record available at https://lccn.loc.gov/2016037124

First Edition

Published in 2017 by
Gareth Stevens Publishing
111 East 14th Street, Suite 349
New York, NY 10003

Copyright © 2017 Gareth Stevens Publishing

Designer: Laura Bowen
Editor: Kristen Nelson

Photo credits: Cover, p. 1 (bee) Lian van den Heever/Gallo Images/Getty Images; cover, pp. 1–24 (background) arigato/Shutterstock.com; cover, pp. 1–24 (corners) Gala/Shutterstock.com; cover, pp. 1–24 (title bar) drada/Shutterstock.com; pp. 1–24 (caption box) Amovitania/Shutterstock.com; pp. 5, 13 Photo Researchers/Science Source/Getty Images; p. 7 Cuan Hansen/Gallo Images/Getty Images; p. 9 SCOTT CAMAZINE/Science Source/Getty Images; p. 11 David Cayless/Photolibrary/Getty Images; p. 15 kosolovskyy/Shutterstock.com; p. 17 bjonesphotography/Shutterstock.com; p. 19 (bee) irin-k/Shutterstock.com; p. 19 (hive) Tony Campbell/Shutterstock.com; p. 20 Botamochy/Shutterstock.com.

Printed in the United States of America

CPSIA compliance information: Batch #CW17GS: For further information contact Gareth Stevens, New York, New York at 1-800-542-2595.

CONTENTS

What's the Buzz? 4

A Big Mistake. 6

The Escape. 8

Bad Bee-haviors 10

A Growing Population 12

Damaging Effects. 14

The Importance of Bees. 16

Problem Solving. 18

Living Together. 20

Glossary. 22

For More Information 23

Index 24

Words in the glossary appear in **bold** type the first time they are used in the text.

WHAT'S THE BUZZ?

Bees are a common sight for most people. They fly around our backyards and gardens, moving from flower to flower. Some even make yummy honey. Perhaps a bee has even stung you...ouch!

What many people don't know is that a kind of bee called the Africanized honeybee can also be found in your neighborhood—and it might do more harm than just stinging. These **aggressive** bees are taking over areas of the United States. There's a real reason why their nickname is "killer bees"!

FIGHT BACK WITH FACTS

Africanized honeybees are an invasive species, which means they're an animal populating areas they're not originally from and causing problems.

The Africanized honeybee may look like an ordinary bee, but it can cause trouble in North and South America!

A BIG MISTAKE

Before the 1950s, the only honeybees in North and South America were European honeybees. Then, a Brazilian scientist named Warwick Kerr traveled to Africa. In 1956, he brought some African honeybees back to Brazil to **breed** with European bees to see if their offspring, or young, could make more honey.

Kerr hoped the offspring would have the European bees' gentleness, too. Then Brazilian beekeepers could use them for a long time to produce more honey.

FIGHT BACK WITH FACTS

Brazil and parts of Africa are tropical, or found in hot areas near the equator. The African bees were used to Brazil's hot weather already!

Kerr brought bees from Africa because South African beekeepers were known to produce a lot of honey from their native bees.

7

THE ESCAPE

In 1957, some African honeybees escaped! At the time, Kerr didn't think they would become such a big problem. He believed the African honeybees would die in the new **environment**. Even if they **mated** with the local honeybees, he thought their offspring would be less aggressive.

The African honeybees did mate with the European honeybees already in Brazil, but Kerr was wrong. Their offspring are the Africanized honeybees—or killer bees—scientists are worried about today. They're an aggressive, fast-moving invasive species.

FIGHT BACK WITH FACTS

Africanized honeybees spread at a rate of 200 to 300 miles (320 to 480 km) per year!

Of the escaped bees, 26 were queens! Queens are the only bees that mate and lay eggs.

BAD BEE-HAVIORS

Africanized honeybees look so much like European honeybees that scientists must do special tests to tell which one a bee is. However, an easier way to tell them apart is by their behavior, or how they act.

African honeybees are much more **defensive** than European honeybees. If they're worried about an animal near their nest, they attack much faster than European honeybees do. African honeybees also attack in groups, or swarms, making them much more dangerous. The Africanized honeybees have taken on these **traits**.

FIGHT BACK WITH FACTS

The first Africanized honeybees spotted in the United States were found in Hidalgo, Texas, in 1990.

The hives of Africanized honeybees can hold as many as 50,000 bees!

11

A GROWING POPULATION

Africanized honeybees are spreading quickly through South America and the southern United States. The weather in these places is similar to what the bees are used to in Africa. Since it's warmer in South America, the bees' population has spread especially fast there.

In addition, it takes less than 3 weeks for their eggs to become full-grown adults, which is faster than European honeybees. Finally, swarms of Africanized honeybees may move 60 miles (97 km) or more at a time and build their nests in many places.

FIGHT BACK WITH FACTS

Africanized honeybees are more resistant to other bugs and diseases that could harm honeybees.

Africanized honeybee colonies also grow in population more quickly than European honeybee colonies. A queen may lay as many as 2,000 eggs a day each spring.

AFRICANIZED HONEYBEE PUPAE

DAMAGING EFFECTS

Killer bees can kill both people and large animals. They don't have more venom, or poison, in their stingers, but a swarm of these invasive bees can sting six to 10 times more than European honeybees! Africanized honeybees attack in larger groups, which means more stings.

These bees also harm the environments in which they live. Since they grow and mate at such a fast rate, there often isn't enough food for all of the bees living in an area with Africanized honeybee colonies.

FIGHT BACK WITH FACTS

Africanized honeybees can sense a threat to their hive from more than 50 feet (15 m) away!

Beekeepers with European honeybees see a drop in the amount of honey the bees can produce whenever Africanized honeybees first invade.

15

THE IMPORTANCE OF BEES

Even though Africanized honeybees cause problems, they're now an important part of their **habitat**. Without bees, even those that are invasive species, we wouldn't be able to have fruits and vegetables.

Bees help fruits and vegetables to grow by pollination, or the moving of pollen from flower to flower. About 90 percent of the pollination of blueberries and cherries depends on honeybees. Almonds depend entirely on honeybees when their flowers need to be pollinated!

FIGHT BACK WITH FACTS

Without pollination, plants wouldn't be able to grow fruits and vegetables, which contain seeds.

Right now, the populations of pollinating bugs like bees are in trouble all over the world. Killer bees may be troublemakers, but we still need them!

BEE POLLINATING A CHERRY TREE

17

PROBLEM SOLVING

There's no way to totally stop the spread of Africanized honeybees. But there might be ways to make them less of a problem. First, beekeepers are continuing to raise European honeybees. Over time, European honeybees breeding with the Africanized honeybees should lessen their aggressive traits. Africanized honeybees are less likely to build hives in places where there are lots of European honeybees, too.

Mostly, governments are trying to make sure people know what to do if they spot killer bees and how to keep from being stung.

FIGHT BACK WITH FACTS

In Central and South America, beekeepers are using killer bees to produce honey just like they hoped to. However, they have to be even more careful than other beekeepers.

BEE SAFE!

Africanized honeybees will chase people or animals they believe to be threats. They'll even wait if you go underwater! So head inside as fast as you can.

IF YOU SEE A BEEHIVE:

- **DON'T** bother it.
- **DO** walk away quickly and tell an adult.

IF A SWARM STARTS TO FLY AFTER YOU:

- **DON'T** swat at the bees.
- **DO** cover your face.
- **DO** run away as fast as you can.
- **DO** go inside and shut the door.
- **DO** call the police so they can get a beekeeper to take care of the swarm.

IF YOU ARE STUNG MANY TIMES:

- **DO** take out all the stingers by scraping them out with your fingernails or the edge of a thick piece of paper.
- **DO** call the doctor or go to a hospital if you feel sick.

LIVING TOGETHER

Africanized honeybees are an invasive species, but they're here to stay. In the United States, they live in much of the Southwest, including Texas and Arizona, as well as parts of Louisiana and southern Florida.

The best way to deal with killer bees is to be careful if you live where they've been found. And if you're scared when you see a beehive, remember: Bees that attack are taking care of their home, just like you are!

Brazil is now one of the top producers of honey in the world!

FIGHT BACK WITH FACTS

Africanized honeybees have been found as far north as North Carolina, but the hives found there were destroyed.

SPREAD OF THE KILLER BEES

Canada

United States

Mexico

WA, OR, ID, MT, ND, MN, WI, MI, MI, ME, VT, NH, MA, NY, RI, CT, NJ, DE, MD, PA, OH, IN, IL, IA, NE, SD, WY, NV, UT, CO, KS, MO, KY, WV, VA, NC, CA, AZ, NM, OK, AR, TN, SC, MS, AL, GA, LA, TX, FL

● Africanized honeybee range

GLOSSARY

aggressive: ready or likely to attack

breed: to mate two animals with desired qualities in order to produce more like them

defensive: having to do with guarding a place and attacking quickly

disease: illness

environment: the conditions that surround a living thing and affect the way it lives

habitat: the natural place where an animal or plant lives

mate: to come together to make babies

resistant: able to survive

threat: something likely to cause harm

trait: a feature that is passed on from parents to children

FOR MORE INFORMATION

Books

Collard, Sneed B. *Science Warriors: The Battle Against Invasive Species.* Boston, MA: Houghton-Mifflin, 2008.

Owings, Lisa. *Killer Bees.* Minneapolis, MN: Bellwether Media, Inc., 2013.

Websites

Invasive Species
nationalgeographic.org/encyclopedia/invasive-species/
Read more about other invasive species and their effects here.

Killer Bees
video.nationalgeographic.com/video/killer_bee
Watch a short video about killer bees and read additional information.

Publisher's note to educators and parents: Our editors have carefully reviewed these websites to ensure that they are suitable for students. Many websites change frequently, however, and we cannot guarantee that a site's future contents will continue to meet our high standards of quality and educational value. Be advised that students should be closely supervised whenever they access the Internet.

INDEX

Africa 6, 7, 12

African honeybees 6, 8, 10

beekeepers 6, 7, 15, 18, 19

Brazil 6, 8, 20

breed 6, 18

Central America 18

colonies 13, 14

European honeybees 6, 8, 10, 12, 13, 14, 15, 18

flowers 4, 16

hives 11, 14, 18, 19, 20

honey 4, 6, 7, 15, 18, 20

invasive 4, 8, 14, 16, 20

Kerr, Warwick 6, 7, 8

North America 5, 6

offspring 6, 8

pollen 16

pollination 16, 17

queens 9, 13

South America 5, 6, 12, 18

sting 4, 14, 18, 19

stingers 14, 19

swarm 10, 12, 14, 19

United States 4, 10, 12, 20

venom 14